Chapter One
Doing What You Don't Want to Do

Aaron pulled into the parking lot of a golf course, so drunk he didn't know where he was or how he got there. He passed out with his car running and didn't wake up until a couple hours later when he heard a tap, tap, tap on the window beside him. It was a sheriff's deputy.

He got out of the car mumbling to himself that he'd done it again. When he'd been released from jail, the last thing he wanted to do was break his probation by drinking and driving. But that's the very thing he did.

Jesse had a history of domestic abuse and sat in a jail cell after hitting his girlfriend over a silly argument. At his sentencing, the prosecutor wanted to put him in prison and throw away the key, but Jesse had a public defender that convinced the judge a furlough to a dual diagnosis facility would be a much better fit. Only there would he get the help he needed to turn his life around.

The judge looked at him and said, "You don't have a good record with drug use and violence. I should probably follow the prosecutor's suggestion, but I'm going to give you one last chance. If I see you before me again, I'll put you in jail for a very long time." Jesse bent over at the waist, shook almost uncontrollably, wept a river of tears, and vowed that the judge wouldn't regret giving him another chance. She'd never see him again.

I talked with Jesse the next day. "You know this is it, right?" I said. "This is your last chance."

He answered, "I understand that. I'll do what's right from now on. You'll not see me here again."

Three weeks later, Jesse was back in jail. He'd lost his temper in the treatment facility and was considered a threat to the other patients. The very thing he wanted to do, he couldn't do. The very thing he didn't want to do, he did.

I met with Bob in an open area of a coffee shop in Buffalo, Minnesota. He told me depression had been a constant companion for many years. I listened as he described his symptoms and told me his life story, but I sensed he'd left out a critical something.

I suggested we meet in a private room in the coffee shop next time, where he broke down and revealed the source of his depression. A sexual perversion had captured him in the crawl space of a house at the age of eight and wouldn't let him go.

"I can't seem to help myself," he said, as he studied the irregular black and white patterns on the table top and shuffled his coffee cup back and forth and round and round. "I just can't."

I have bad news and good news for you," I said. The bad news is you *can't* help yourself. You're right in that.

"Bob's head moved down closer to the table top, and I could now hear the movement of his coffee-cup as well as see it.

I smiled. "Do you want the good news now, Bob?"

His head came up. "Boy do I."

"*You* can't help yourself but I know Someone who can." Bob was a churchgoer but hadn't accepted Jesus Christ as his Savior and Lord. On the whiteboard in the

Stop Doing What You Don't Want to Do

I know that all God's commands are spiritual, but I'm not...I'm full of myself—after all, I've spent a long time in sin's prison. What I don't understand about myself is that I decide one way, but then I act another, doing things I absolutely despise.

I need something more! If the power of sin within me keeps sabotaging my best intentions, I obviously need help! I realize that I don't have what it takes. I can will it, but I can't do it. I decide to do good, but I don't really do it; I decide not to do bad, but then I do it anyway.

It happens so regularly that it's predictable. The moment I decide to do good, sin is there to trip me up. I truly delight in God's commands, but it's pretty obvious that not all of me joins in that delight. Parts of me covertly rebel, and just when I least expect it, they take charge.

I've tried everything and nothing helps. I'm at the end of my rope. Is there no one who can do anything for me? Isn't that the real question?

The answer, thank God, is that Jesus Christ can and does. Romans 7: 14-25 (The Message)

Copyright © 2019 by Patrick Day

Minneapolis, Minnesota
patrickday@pyramidpublishers.com

All rights reserved. No part of this publication may be reproduced, stored in a retrieval system, or transmitted, in any form or by any means, electronic, mechanical, photocopying, recording, or otherwise, without the prior written permission of the author.

Printed by Lightning Source
1246 Heil Quaker Blvd. La Vergne, TN USA 37086
ISBN – 978-0-9982014-6-7

Unless otherwise noted, scripture quotations are from The Holy Bible, New International Version®, NIV®. Copyright © 1973, 1978, 1984, 2011 by Biblica, Inc.™ Used by permission of Zondervan.

Cover Design by Myron Sahlberg
Drawings by James Nelson
Interior Design by Just Ink Digital Design
Printed in the United States of America

meeting room, I drew the chart you'll find in the third chapter of this book and explained the ABCs of salvation.

Bob prayed to accept Jesus into his heart, and his life changed from darkness to light. Within months, he was freed from depression and freed from the bondage of his sexual perversion.

These three case studies have very different endings. We'll meet Aaron again in Chapter Five and see how his life turned around when he stopped having Jesus follow Him and let Him play the lead role in their life together. Bob found freedom when he became saved and let Jesus speak into the soul of his sexual perversion and depression and heal him of both. Jesse could never put anyone in front of Jesse. He claimed he was a Christian but he never put Christ first in his life.

Is there something that holds you captive? An addiction you can't shake – drugs, alcohol, pornography, gambling? Criminal behavior that returns you to jail again and again – substance abuse, violence, theft, impulsive conduct?

Let me tell you, your situation is not hopeless and you're not helpless. God can help you do what you've not been able to do on your own in the past. Read on and find hope.

You are my hiding place; you will protect me from trouble. Psalm 32:7

Chapter Two
Who Are You?

Who are you that the Lord would know your name, would know your inner heart, and would be sad when you are hurting? To Him, you are not the addicted one or the one who can't stay out of jail. Never mind that others refer to you as a drunk or a criminal? He calls you His son or daughter, and He cares deeply about you.

Even your family may give up on you, but He won't, ever. He knows what a hard life you've had. He understands why you turn to drugs and crime. In Matthew 11:28, Jesus says, *Come to me, all you who are weary and burdened, and I will give you rest.*

Listen as He speaks to you in Isaiah 43:1-5.

Fear not, for I have redeemed you;
I have called you by name; you are mine.
When you pass through the waters,
I will be with you;
and when you pass through the rivers,
they will not sweep over you.
When you walk through the fire,
you will not be burned;
the flames will not set you ablaze.
For I am the LORD your God,
the Holy One of Israel, your Savior ... You
are precious and honored in my sight,
and ... I love you.

Even if everyone else rejects you, He won't. No matter how many times you fail, He's ready to take you back just the way you are, ready to give you another chance. He'll never say to you, "Well, that's it. I'm going to wash my hands of you." Let's listen as Jesus tells the story of the prodigal son in Luke 15:11-32 (*The Message*).

There was once a man who had two sons. The younger said to his father, "Father, I want right now what's coming to me."

So the father divided the property between them. It wasn't long before the younger son packed his bags and left for a distant country. There, undisciplined and dissipated, he wasted everything he had. After he had gone through all his money, there was a bad famine all through that country and he began to hurt. He signed on with a citizen there who assigned him to his fields to slop the pigs. He was so hungry he would have eaten the corncobs in the pig slop, but no one would give him any.

That brought him to his senses. He said, "All those farmhands working for my father sit down to three meals a day, and here I am starving to death. I'm going back to my father. I'll say to him, Father, I've sinned against God, I've sinned before you; I don't deserve to be called your son. Take me on as a hired hand." He got right up and went home to his father.

When he was still a long way off, his father saw him. His heart pounding, he ran out, embraced him, and kissed him. The son started his speech: "Father, I've sinned against God, I've sinned before you; I don't deserve to be called your son ever again."

But the father wasn't listening. He was calling to the servants, "Quick. Bring a clean set of clothes and dress him. Put the family ring on his finger and sandals on his feet. Then get a grain-fed heifer and roast it. We're going to feast! We're going to have a wonderful time! My son is here—given up for dead and now alive! Given up for lost and now found!' And they began to have a wonderful time.

You may have packed your bags for a distant country, so to speak. The addiction you've fallen victim to is that distant country, as is the jail cell you may be sitting in. Your obsession with all things sexual is not the country where your Father lives, nor is your confessing to the same sins over and over again.

When you are fed up with your present life, as was the prodigal son, you can set out to come back to your Father. He's waiting for you. Maybe you don't yet have a personal relationship with His Son, Jesus Christ, the One who died for your sins. Come to the Father's kingdom, and He'll give you His Son to show you His ways and teach you His paths. Maybe you have accepted Jesus as your Savior and Lord, but you left

Him behind when you went to the land of addictions or jail.

Jesus waits for you in the kingdom of His Father here on earth. He'll welcome you with open arms. He'll cry for the hard life you've led and promise you something so much better. He'll give you His Holy Spirit to encourage you and lead you down a path of sobriety, freedom from jail or prison, and the release of obsessions that have you tied up in a knot.

Pack up all your cares and woes in a duffle bag and throw it at the feet of Jesus. Let Him take care of it because you already know you can't. Tell Him you want to live in His kingdom for the rest of your life, and He'll protect you and give you peace and a meaningful life.

Then look up to your Father in heaven and hear Him say, "Welcome home my son. Welcome home my daughter. I have good things planned for you. I will never leave you nor forsake you."

Let's look at something called switching addictions. Deciding to retire from your addiction hasn't worked because you leave a space in your life that demands to be filled. You can't escape it. You're addictive by nature and you're going to be addicted to one thing or another. Instead of fighting the addiction that seems to always get the upper hand, switch from one addiction to another. Become addicted to Jesus Christ and crave Him as much as you used to crave alcohol or drugs.

I will instruct you and teach you in the way you should go; I will counsel you with my loving eye on you. Psalm 32:8

Chapter Three
What Does It Mean to Be Saved?

To be saved means someone needs to be rescued, as in you. If you don't think you need to be rescued, if you're satisfied with your life the way it is, then you should close this book and start playing video games.

To be saved means turning away *from* a life that is without God, that is focused solely upon yourself. Being saved also means being saved from destructive patterns of life – things that destroy you instead of build you up. Some of those common destructive things are alcohol, drugs, sexual abuse and misuse, anger, lust for power, pursuit of money at the expense of others, and so forth.

How you get saved isn't rocket science. The chart and explanation below give you the nuts and the bolts.

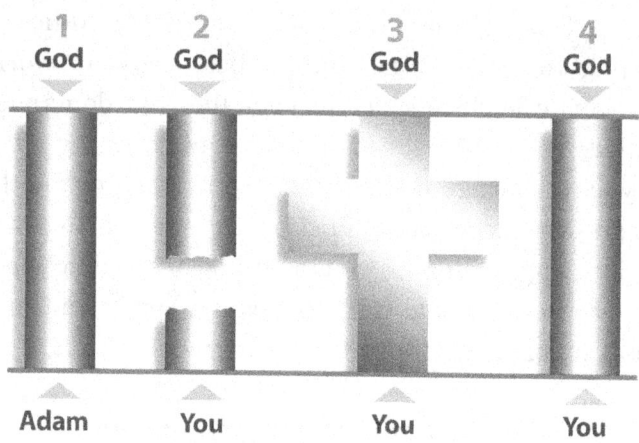

1. IN THE BEGINNING ADAM AND EVE HAD A DIRECT CONNECTION TO GOD. They walked with Him and talked with Him and knew that He was their

own. All was good, and they would never die. It's how God meant it to be. But God didn't want them to be robots, so He gave them a free will to love and obey Him, or not. Adam and Eve are our original ancestors, and we inherit all that they were – body, soul, spirit ... and sin. The soul is our inner self, who we are. The spirit is our innermost self, where God lives in us.

2. ADAM AND EVE BROKE THE CONNECTION when they made a new friend in the garden and listened to Satan instead of God. When they chose to eat fruit from the Tree of the Knowledge of Good and Evil, in direct disobedience to God's command not to do so, sin entered the world and separated them from God.

Guess what? Not only did they ruin it for themselves, they ruined it for us as well. We all come into the world with their sinful nature and a natural tendency to go our own way, just like they did. We also come into the world with a knowledge of God and a desire to connect with Him. But whatever we do on our own isn't good enough. If it were, there would have been no reason for Jesus to die on the cross for our sins. There's a debt to be paid (the first side of salvation), and all the wealth in the world won't pay it off. We're all doomed to debtors prison, also known as hell.

Some people try to do more good than bad, but that's like pouring pure water into a cesspool. Other folks pray up a storm to get saved, but only end up with sore knees and a bad back. Attending church in the hopes of being saved has as much chance of happening as a starving person being renewed who goes into a banquet room and never touches the food.

So we're all doomed to eternal separation? Not quite.

3. GOD HAS A WONDERFUL PLAN FOR US. Though *we* can't bridge the gap, God did it for us by sending Jesus Christ to earth to take away the sinful nature (the second side of salvation) Adam and Eve stuck us with. As an added bonus, He also takes away all the sins we've ever committed. So now what? Well, every one of us stands between 2 and 3 on the chart. I call that the choosing spot. We can look over to Adam and Eve and say, "Hey, I guess I'll do it your way." *Or* we can look to the cross of Jesus and say, "Lord, I desire with all my heart to do it Your way. The one is death and the other is life.

The simple way this plan works is that Jesus is the giver and you are the taker. Both parts need to take place, but how?

4. JESUS WILL PAY YOUR DEBT IF YOU ACCEPT HIM AS YOUR SAVIOR AND LORD. That's how you become re-connected with God. Now you're in the banquet room, surrounded by food and drink that is endless. You're so hungry you don't know how you're going to make it one more hour, and He tells you to dig in.

But you still have a choice to make. You need to accept his invitation to chow down on a steak or vegetarian delight. And you need to pull the levers on the drinks dispenser to choose, milk, fruit punch, or pure spring water from the deepest wells. Soon you'll be so full that you'll want to settle in for a long nap.

You're ready, but you may not know the secret formula for making that choice. Actually, it's not a secret formula. It's as simple as ABC.

A. ADMIT your natural self in Adam is hopelessly corrupt and needs redemption. ADMIT you have been a sinful creature from the day you were born.

B. BELIEVE Jesus is the Way and the Truth and the Life, just like He said He was in John 14. BELIEVE He died on the cross so a wretch like you can have your sins forgiven and pick up a passport for heaven (the third side of salvation).

C. CHOOSE Jesus Christ as Savior and ask Him to be the Lord of your life. CHOOSE to give Him your addictions, obsessions, and criminal behavior and do for you what you can't do for yourself.

It's this choosing part that's most important. But it's not a choice you make in your mind or with your emotions. You make it with your will – to choose one thing instead of the other. Then grace comes flooding in.

For it is by grace you have been saved, through faith, and this not of yourselves, it is the gift of God. Ephesians 2:8&9

Isn't it a wonderful thing to know you can be saved? This calls for a celebration. But don't put the balloons out yet, for without a choice, there is no salvation. The good news is before you, but you need to grab it.

Let me give you an example. Cyanide is a lethal poison. You know that. But just knowing it will kill you won't cause you any harm. Or feeling a dread when you look at the bottle won't cause you to die. No, only if you grab the bottle with your hand and put it to your lips and drink it will it kill you.

In the same way, knowing Jesus came to save you from the sin nature you were born with and all the sins you have committed yourself won't do you any good. You need to choose to accept Him into your heart.

In John 6:54, Jesus says,

Whoever eats My flesh and drinks My blood has eternal life, and I will raise him up on the last day.

This is about as direct a comparison to the bottle of cyanide as you'll find. What Jesus is saying here is that you can only enter into the Kingdom of Heaven if you take Him into the very heart of your being. Just as taking food and liquids into your body give you natural life, so taking Jesus into your spirit and soul give you spiritual life.

Chapter Four
Putting a Stop to the Endless Cycle

God doesn't see you as a person who's addicted or in jail. He sees you as His son or daughter, if you choose to walk with Him.

"But I *am* walking with Him," you might say. That's wonderful, but make sure He's leading and you're following, or you'll find yourself in a pickle.

You can't add Christ to your life like putting butter on your bread or frosting on your cake. It won't work if you give Him a small room in the basement of your soul that you visit every now and again – your soul being your inner self, the one-of-a kind you.

This drawing shows the cycle of recidivism – a life without God or with Christ in the basement.

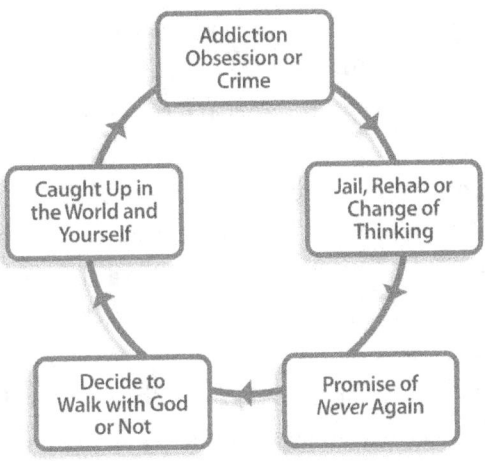

You'll only become free when Christ is the butter *and* the bread, the frosting *and* the cake, and the whole house of your life. This is how you break the cycle.

Let's say you decide to walk with God and let Christ lead you. Wonderful! But Christianity is not a matter of taking a first step on a short path and then sitting down on a bench to rest. There's a long journey ahead of you, and you need to be prepared for it.

The Apostle Paul spent three years in a desert preparing for his ministry. In the same way, you need time apart to learn who Jesus is and why He came to earth, a separation from everyday life, so to speak. Time in jail will work...or a stay at a Christian rehab facility like Adult and Teen Challenge...or a long retreat away from home...or set-apart times each day for a year or so.

You're still not done after the separation. You need the drip, drip, drip of the Holy Spirit to nurture your soul every day or you'll dry up like a raisin in the sun. If you're a bit impatient and want to know what the dripping is all about, turn to Chapter Eleven.

Early in my ministry, I gave a talk to 18 inmates in a county jail in central Minnesota. At one point, I said matter-of-factly, "Some of you have been in jail five times or ten times or maybe even twenty times."

A man who sat in the front row spoke up in a wobbly voice, "Try 50 times." I was stunned and couldn't speak for what seemed like a very long time, though the length of my silence could probably have been measured in seconds. I thought to myself, "I've given these men general information. Now it's personal."

Slowly I regained my composure and spoke *with* these men instead of *at* them. "Are you guys mainly Christians?" I asked. Heads nodded, including the man of 50 jail sentences.

"How many of you read the Bible every day?" Hands went up. "How many pray regularly in here?" More hands. "Do you attend church services and sign up for Christian groups like the Gideons?" They all said yes. "Do you hang around fellow believers in your cell blocks?" They became more enthusiastic as they all raised their hands. It was now my turn to stun them.

"Then why do you keep committing the same crimes and keep coming back to jail?" If their enthusiasm a minute before were a balloon, I had just popped it.

They looked at me for an answer to the question they'd asked themselves hundreds of times.

"You may have found Jesus in jail or strengthened your relationship with Him. You've had the time and opportunity here to stay tuned to Jesus Christ through the power of the Holy Spirit. Think of your inner life as a radio station dial. The Holy Spirit station is 160, and the featured song is *In Christ Alone*. The World/Self station is 55 and the featured song is *I Did It My Way*.

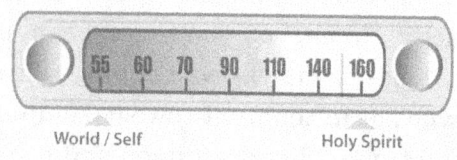

World / Self   Holy Spirit

"The closer you are to 160, the safer you are. The closer to 55, the more danger you're in. If you do nothing to stay near 160, you slowly drift back toward 55. You promise yourself it will be different this time when you get out. You'll stay tuned to Jesus. But you've made that promise before and you've broken that promise before, some of you up to 50 times.

"When you get out of jail, you become distracted with family, friends, finding a job, and all the other stuff coming at you 100 miles an hour in the real world. You get slapped in the face with troubles and woes. You can barely hear *In Christ Alone* if you hear it at all.

"You no longer have the time to stay tuned to the Holy Spirit station, and so you drift to the station where the ways of the world and your own wants play so loudly that you lose touch with the Jesus you heard so clearly in jail. He still calls out to you, but you can't hear Him because there's more of you and the world in your life than there is of Him. There's also Adam and Eve's old friend from the Garden who takes his best shot at tempting you when Jesus is not nearby to protect you. *That*, my friends, is the answer to the question of how you can be a believer and end up back in jail over and over again." I saw flickers of light peeking through on the faces of several of the men.

"Without being near the Holy Spirit station, where Jesus and His Father are the music, you meander back to the World/Self station where temptations fly at you like a colony of bats. In a moment of stress or desperation, you down a double shot of whisky or share a snort of crystal meth. Then it's off to the races. Or in a fit of anger, you'll hit someone. Or you'll steal enough money to pay the bills. Or you'll cave in to your sexual desires just one time." All faces now lit up.

"You want to avoid that, right?" Every head went up and down. "So what are you going to do?" I was met by blank stares and silence. "I'm going to tell you about seven practical things you can do to stay close to Jesus. Are you ready?" All heads nodded in eager anticipation. You may have already sneaked a peek at Chapter Eleven, which is where I went next.

The point of all this is that you are a slave to one master or another. Will you be a slave to drugs, alcohol, or criminal behavior? Or will you be a slave to Jesus?

*Don't you know that when you offer yourselves to someone as obedient **slaves**, you are **slaves** of the one you obey—whether you are **slaves** to sin, which leads to death, or to obedience, which leads to righteousness?* Romans 6:16

Chapter Five
On the Road Again

Aaron loved Jesus, but he couldn't walk away from his alcoholism. He'd get arrested for DWI and tossed into jail. There he'd become involved in every Christian program available and convince himself that Jesus would help him to never drink again. After serving his time, he'd make it a few days, maybe, before he returned to his best friend and constant companion – a bottle of vodka. One day on the outside, in a drunken brawl, he stabbed his best friend and ended up in a state prison. He'd call me from there and weep and beg me to help him stay sober.

Aaron was released into intensive supervised release but couldn't handle the restrictions. One day he walked away to the nearest bar and started pouring down drinks like there was no tomorrow. That violated his probation, and I met him in jail for the second time.

"What are we going to do about this?" I asked Aaron.

He hung his head in shame. "I don't know. Nothing I do works. I guess I'm just a hopeless drunk."

"You're a believer, Aaron, right?"

"You know I am, Pat."

"Yes, I know that. What do you think God's will is for you?

Aaron looked puzzled. "Stay out of jail? Stop drinking?"

"Well, yes, but that's not the starting point. He wants a personal relationship with you on His terms. That's His underlying will."

Aaron sniffled and spoke out of years of frustration, "You know I've accepted Jesus into my heart, Pat. So I'm living in His will right? Then why can't I stop drinking? I've asked Jesus a thousand times to help me stop, but it doesn't do any good." At this point, Aaron broke down and couldn't say any more.

His honesty and desperation moved me. I prayed silently for the Holy Spirit to show me what to say next. Aaron bowed his head in sorrow and waited. It was as if time stood still.

"Do you feel you are walking with Jesus, Aaron?" I spoke out of my spirit, unsure where this was heading.

His head popped up and his voice came out in smoldering frustration. "I read the Bible every day, Pat. I pray every day. I love Jesus and want to walk with Him all the time. What else do I need to do?"

As I prayed for wisdom, a picture came into my mind.

I got up and walked over to a whiteboard and drew as best I could what the Holy Spirit had shown me.

"Yes, Aaron, I believe you're walking on the road of your life with Jesus, but I think you're in the wrong place on that road." Then I turned around to face him.

Aaron looked like he'd just been slapped across the face by the Holy Spirit. I could almost see the wheels in his mind grinding away.

"The first road is you before you were saved – on your own. The second road is you right now. You've been saved, but you're determined to go your own way and ask Jesus for help here and there. The third road is the way God wants you to live – putting Jesus before you and following Him where He wants you to go.

"On the second road, you say, 'Aaron is most important.' On the third road you say, 'Jesus is most important.' The difference between the two is life changing."

Aaron blurted out in excitement, "I see it. I see it. I'm walking down the wrong road. Or should I say I'm on the right road but in the wrong place. Tell me more."

The Holy Spirit led me in what to tell this eager beaver. "You're correct when you say you're on the right road but in the wrong place. You're treating Jesus like a little puppy dog who follows you to do your bidding. "Jesus, help me with my drinking. Jesus, keep me out of jail."

Aaron now looked confused. "What's wrong with that? Isn't that what Jesus is supposed to do, help us with our troubles?"

"That's not the way it works with Jesus, Aaron. You need to let Him lead and you follow. He knows the road better than you do. He knows where He wants you to go, and you don't. Instead of saying, 'Jesus help me with my drinking,' say, 'Jesus, I want to follow You wherever You go.' Do you think Jesus would lead you into a bar you're walking past?"

Aaron laughed. "No way." I could see by the look on his face that he got it. "And if I'm reaching for a bottle of vodka at home, what do I do?"

The Holy Spirit had him. "Ask Jesus if he'd like to sit down with you and share the bottle."

Aaron laughed again. "No way He'd wanna to do that."

"Then you don't either. You see the two of you are a team on the road of your life. *He* wants to be your best friend and constant companion, not a bottle of vodka. But you have to let Him lead as the Lord and Master of your life...and you follow. You are to walk alongside Him – but a half step behind, close enough to talk with Him but letting there be no doubt who is leading and who is following.

Aaron slammed his hand on the table with such a bang that it startled me. "I'll do it. No more puppy-dog Jesus. I'll follow Him into hell if that's what He wants."

I laughed. "I don't think He'd take you there, Aaron, but you have the idea. Or maybe He will take you through a kind of hell in this life."

"That's what I meant," Aaron said. A smile draped his face.

Aaron is out of jail now and I pray he's following Jesus past bars and drinking soda water with Him. *That's* God's will for him.

Chapter Six
From Gang Member to Christian

Mitch was once a member of La Mara Salvatrucha, also known as MS-13, a notorious international gang involved in drug dealing and violence. One day when he was in Mexico, he witnessed a rival gang member literally shot in half with an AK-47 assault weapon. The upper half of the torso reached out to grab an imaginary something for a couple of seconds before it ceased moving. That image became seared into Mitch's memory and reappeared in living color during restless nights.

Mitch left the gang shortly after that incident but still lived in a world of violence and drugs. He used meth heavily and sold it on the streets for a gang out of St. Paul. Eventually, he ended up in jail, and that's where I met him at a Sunday afternoon Gideon Bible study. As I looked at him sitting in a chair to my left, the Holy Spirit planted a thought into my mind that this guy needed help and I should meet with him one-on-one, which I did.

Both his parents were Hell's Angels members and had biker get-togethers in their front yard during his younger years. His mother left when Mitch was eight-years-old, and he ended up in a homeless shelter with his father, a violent man who beat his own brother to death in a drunken brawl. Mitch then lived with his grandmother who brought some stability into his life until his mother, a prostitute who worked truck stops, came in the dead of night to take him away to Texas. There he started smoking meth at the age of 14.

After his first bust for drugs, Mitch signed up for a Boot Camp program that turned him around. For ten years after that, he lived a law-abiding and sober lifestyle and got some religion in the bargain. Then his old lifestyle caught up with him and, as he told me, he was so wasted on using meth himself, selling it to his clients 24-hours a day, and not eating or sleeping for long stretches of time, that his skin turned a chalky gray and he'd have died if he hadn't been arrested for possession of stolen property.

During our second session together, I asked Mitch if he wanted freedom from his addiction and life of crime. He nodded. I explained God's plan of salvation and asked if he wanted to give his life over to Jesus Christ.

"What other choice do I have, Pat? If I'm paroled and let out, I'll go right back to using and selling. If I'm not killed by rival gangs in a drug war, I'll die of an overdose or from my body shutting down. I don't know anything different."

I went to the whiteboard against the wall and drew out the chart from Chapter Three. Then I covered with Mitch the ABCs prayer of salvation. One critical point for anyone reading this to understand clearly – I can't save anyone by what I show and explain. I'm only a tool for the work of the Holy Spirit.

Sometimes I do the drawing and explaining and am met with blank stares or glimmerings of understanding but no conversion. With Mitch, after he prayed to receive Jesus Christ as his Savior and Lord, I could tell that he had been truly born-again into a personal relationship with Jesus. Not a knowledge of Him but an embracing of Him, a surrender of his will to His will. He was a new creation, and he knew it.

We met several more times to study the Bible and talk about his future on the outside with Christ within him and the power of the Holy Spirit guiding him to freedom from crime and addiction.

The last time I saw Mitch he had made application to an Adult and Teen Challenge for their 13-month program. "I need a separation from my life of crime and drug use. I'm afraid if I go out there again, I'll go back to my old ways. I need time with the Lord to learn how to live my new life."

I have prayed for Mitch since then and hope to see him again when I give chapel at the Adult and Teen Challenge where he's at in Minnesota. It's happened that way before.

One of the most revealing passages in the Bible that tells what our relationship with Jesus Christ is to be is John 15: 5-6. Mitch was a branch laying on the roadside about to be picked up and thrown into the fire until he became grafted, through the power of the Holy Spirit, into the True Vine – Jesus Christ.

I am the vine; you are the branches. If you remain in Me and I in you, you will bear much fruit; apart from Me you can do nothing. If you do not remain in Me, you are like a branch that is thrown away and withers; such branches are picked up, thrown into the fire and burned

Chapter Seven
Stacie's Lesson

One day in late November, when the temperature outside was more like September, I met with Stacie for the third time. Her story sounded like something out of a Greek tragedy – molested, raped, battered, meth addict, children taken away, a series of bad relationships, and fearful of what would happen next.

She had accepted Jesus a couple of years before we met but had distorted thoughts about His role in her life, caused most likely by the meth she wolfed down and the disasters that had swept over her. She pleaded and begged with Jesus to help her in her troubles, but nothing changed. She had been saved, but she hadn't been transformed into the woman God wanted her to be – dependent on Him and following Him and trusting in Him alone, not in the world or the people surrounding her.

"Let's look at John 14:31," I said to her after a bit of chit-chat about the weather and how she felt that day.

Rise, let us go away from here.

Stacie lifted her head and looked directly at me. "Why'd you pick that verse? It don't mean nuthin to me."

I smiled. "Oh, it will Stacie. It will. Let's look at what's happening in John 14 at that time. Jesus and the twelve apostles were reclining around a table where the Last Supper took place. Jesus was telling them about

Himself and the Holy Spirit whom He would soon send to them. Then Jesus stood up and invited them to get up as well and follow Him."

"What's the point?" Stacie asked with a blank look.

I smiled again. OK, Stacie, let's get to the point."

She settled back in her chair with her arms folded across her chest. "When Jesus rose, the apostles followed Him to the Mount of Olives where He continued to talk to them. They didn't go off on their own asking Jesus to help them on their path in life. They followed Him without question, having no clue that Jesus would be arrested there and taken off to be killed on a Roman cross.

"You see, Stacie, that's the way it is with you and me. We are to rise up with Jesus as He goes about His business in our lives. We are not to rise up and go about our own affairs and somehow think He will follow us, on the fringes of our lives, so to speak."

I have seen the look that came over Stacie's face many times before – the look of an awakening to a new way of seeing life, the revealing of something never thought of before.

"I see it, Pat," Stacie said in a voice that quivered with excitement. "I've been tryin to figure things out and all the mistakes I've made and askin Jesus to help me out. It drives me crazy. Now you're tellin me all I need do is follow Jesus and let Him figure it out."

When someone realizes the truth of Christianity, I get pretty excited myself. I wanted to jump out of my chair, raise my hands in jubilation, and shout "hallelujah." But I didn't. Instead, I simply said, "You've got it, Stacie. Now what are you going to do with it?"

"You tell me," she said, with a smile on her face.

"OK, read Chapter 1 in the gospel of John and then chapters 14, 15, and 16. Those chapters will tell you who Jesus is and why He came to earth. Then you'll know who it is you're following."

"I'll do it," she said, with a conviction in her voice that convinced me that's exactly what she'd do."

"We'll talk about those chapters when we meet next week." I prayed over Stacie and she left the room to be replaced by another inmate who had seen the truth a couple weeks before.

When I met with Stacie a week later, she skipped into the conference room and was practically jumping up and down with joy. I became caught up in her enthusiasm and asked, "Who are you, Stacie?"

She cried tears of happiness. "I've read the chapters in John that you gave me and I now *know* who I am. I'm a child of God." To prove her point, she read John 1:12.

Yet to all who did receive Him, to those who believed in His name, he gave the right to become children of God — children born not of natural descent, nor of human decision or a husband's will, but born of God.

Chapter Eight
The Secret of a Joyful Life

Michael shuffled into a Gideon Bible Study one Sunday afternoon just when I asked who of the four people already seated were born-again believers. He turned to me and said he wanted to be saved, but he had to forgive himself first of his terrible sin. I found out later the sin and crime was criminal sexual conduct in the first degree.

I told Michael, "I've got good news for you. You can't forgive yourself. Only God can do that." Since some of the others had also indicated they were not believers, I went through the plan of salvation on the whiteboard at the front of the room and prayed the ABCs of salvation with them [See Chapter Three]. When I looked up, Michael had his hands palm up on his knees, and the look on his face had turned from hopeless to glowing. I had not witnessed such a physical manifestation of salvation before.

I met with Michael several times while he was still in jail and now talk to him by phone at least once a month and visit him in prison once a year. He's serving an eight-year sentence for his crime but has been delivered from his sin and, I believe with all my heart, will not offend ever again when he is released. You see, Jesus set him free from his sexual bondage, and he now only wants to serve Him for the rest of his life. I can honestly say he's one of the most solid Christians I know.

I know non-Christians and Christians alike who are so terribly unhappy because of money problems, relationship problems, troubles at work, and even unrest in the churches they attend. And yet Michael is joyful in his faith though he's serving an eight-year sentence. And Shawn is joyful even though he's serving 26 years in a state prison.

On June 1, 2016, Shawn Tyler Benson, a reckless drug addict, living in a meth house, was ordered by the owner of the house to put two bullets in the back of a young woman's head, execution style, because he thought she was about to snitch on all of them. Shawn, still a bit high on meth, didn't want to do something like that. Then the owner pulled out a hypodermic needle filled with meth and asked if Shawn wanted to be mainlined.

I asked Shawn later why he allowed himself to be shot up with meth. He answered with a cheerless laugh. "You've got to remember, I was a hopeless meth addict. Of course I wanted more meth. I just didn't realize how much more he was shooting into me."

Two hours later, in a park south of Buffalo, Minnesota, Shawn put a bullet into the back of the head of the woman as she lay on the ground bleeding, already shot three times by another member of the meth house who drove the execution car. Later that same day, everyone in the house escaped to Northern Minnesota where they were eventually arrested and taken to the Wright County Jail.

For his first four months in jail, as Shawn said, "My life was a train wreck. I thought I would go insane. I was looking for ways to kill myself, but I was on suicide watch and a guard came by my cell every few minutes."

Then one day a book cart came by, and Shawn pulled out a pocket New Testament provided by the Gideons, of which I am one. He turned to the book of John and started reading, he doesn't remember where, when suddenly the Holy Spirit revealed to him his need for saving and that Jesus Christ was the only way. He chose Jesus as his Savior and Lord that very minute, and his life turned from the terrors of night to a bright and shining day. He was the happiest guy in the jail for almost two years until his sentencing. The other inmates asked how he could be so joyful when he might spend the rest of his life in jail. He said, "Because I know Who will be there with me."

> *Here I am! I stand at the door and knock. If anyone hears my voice and opens the door, I will come in and eat with him, and he with Me.*
> Revelation 3:20

The secret of a joyful life is to open the door of your life to Jesus. That doesn't mean everything will turn up roses for you, but Jesus will be with you no matter what you are going through. You never have to wonder if he's there. He's told you He is, and He's told you He will be with you in all your troubles.

In this world you will have trouble. But take heart! I have overcome the world. John 16.33

Say to yourself or scream it from the mountaintops. "I choose Jesus as my Lord. I choose to obey His commands as I find them in the Bible. I choose to go His way instead of my way. I choose to open the door of my soul to His light and guidance."

Simply put your will over on God's side, making up your mind that you will believe what He says because He says it.

Though He slay me, yet will I hope in Him. Job 13:15

Chapter Nine
Andrew's Story

Andrew never missed a Gideons Sunday afternoon Bible study in the Wright County Jail. He'd bring with him a Bible that looked like it had 20 years of hard use on it, even though he'd gotten it new less than a year before. As we discussed a passage from Scripture, different inmates would give an opinion of what it meant to them based on their knowledge and experience. Not Andrew. He'd open his Bible and read a verse or verses from elsewhere in the Word that shed light on what we were talking about. And when he read, the other inmates became silent and listened to him as if he were their teacher.

One Sunday, he had the group read all of Romans 8. Then he explained how it related to what we were discussing. My partner and I laughed on the way out of the jail. Andrew had hijacked the Bible study and did a better job than we had.

I figured I needed to learn more about this guy and started meeting with him at the jail in my role as a chaplain. Andrew was such a solid Christian and so knowledgeable of the Bible that I learned as much from him as he did from me.

After the Apostle Paul's conversion, he disappeared into the desert for three years during which time the Holy Spirit instructed him in the ways of the Lord, from which he emerged ready to communicate divine truth. I felt something similar to that happened to Andrew in the past year, as he spent hours and hours studying

Scripture in the quiet of his cell and listening for the instruction of the Holy Spirit.

Andrew had pled guilty to 3rd degree burglary, a crime he committed when he was so wasted on drugs that he thought he was entering his own garage. He told me he didn't want to serve out his time and be released. He wanted to be furloughed to Adult and Teen Challenge because he knew that was his best chance to get his life together. He knew he couldn't be freed from his addiction on his own.

On a crisp Tuesday morning in November, I drove up to another county where the sentencing for Andrew took place. I thought it would be a mere formality that Andrew would be furloughed to serve out his sentence at Adult and Teen Challenge, a Christian facility that has an incredible success rate with drug addicts and criminals.

But the prosecuting attorney wanted none of it. If it were up to him, Andrew would go to jail for the rest of his life. He spoke forcefully to the judge that Andrew didn't deserve a furlough. He could get the help he needed in jail (I couldn't believe he said that). Now Andrew has a bit of a temper, but he was meek in his statement. "I did wrong in what I did and deserve the sentence I have. I'm just asking to get the help I need to stay off drugs." He didn't say much else other than that. The judge pondered what the prosecutor had said and what Andrew had said.

As I sat there waiting for the judge to pronounce sentence, I didn't give Andrew much of a chance. My experience has been that judges in these cases usually follow through on the recommendation of the county prosecutor. I wondered how Andrew would handle being sent back to jail to finish out his sentence. All he wanted to talk about when we met was how Jesus had turned his life around and how he wanted to serve Him in whatever way Jesus wanted him to, even if that meant serving his time out in jail and heading out into an unknown future.

I looked up from my thoughts because the judge was about to speak. She reduced his sentence to one year and agreed to let him be furloughed to Adult and Teen Challenge. What an amazing God to engineer what was the very best for Andrew! As I left the courtroom, I was reminded of 1 Samuel 2:30.

Those who honor Me I will honor.

Chapter Ten
The Battle is Never Over

Fourteen times Tyler went through rehab at one place or another. Fourteen times he went right back to drugs and alcohol. Meth was his drug of choice.

In the course of time, his alcohol and drug addictions became so out of control that he lost his job, girlfriend, dog, and house...and took up residence in four different jails in two states.

I met him at a Sunday afternoon Gideons Bible study in the Wright County Jail. The Holy Spirit prompted me to ask Tyler if wanted to meet with me when he was released. He did.

We met at a coffee shop the following Friday, and I mainly listened to Tyler's story. We met one more time, but he never made our scheduled third meeting because he had taken off on a two-week alcohol and meth binge. He lived out of his car and committed a burglary and a theft in order to buy booze, drugs, and some food.

Tyler sank so low that he decided to end his life by standing on a track and waiting for a train to run over him. Somehow his mother and sister found him and hauled him off to a hospital in Minneapolis.

He called me from the hospital and told me he'd reached bottom and was ready to turn his life around. I said, "You've tried that before and couldn't stay sober. You can't do it on your own."

There was a long pause on the other end of the line before he asked, "What can I do then?"

"You need to meet the real Jesus," I answered, not thoughts about Him you have in your mind. Go into your room, open your Bible, and ask to see Jesus.

The next morning he called me all excited and told me about his encounter the previous evening. "It's hard to explain. I didn't see Jesus in a vision or hear an audible voice, but I knew without a doubt it was Jesus.

"I felt His presence and heard inside me a quiet voice that said, 'It will be all right, son.' I felt God's love rain down on me. I cried without tears."

After he was released from the hospital, he went to a Christian-based rehab facility called Metro Hope Center and spent 14 months becoming grounded in his Christian faith and turning from his way to God's way.

When he left Metro Hope, he got a job as a fiber optic technician laying high-speed cable to rural areas. For almost a year, he attended two church services each Sunday, attended Celebrate Recovery meetings every week, had an AA Sponsor, got up two hours early every morning for Scripture reading and prayer, and only listened to Christian radio stations.

Tyler and I talked at least twice a week, and I was pleased with his dedication and passion in making his life all about Jesus.

I wish that were the end of Tyler's story. One afternoon, during a regular phone call, Tyler told me he wanted to start up a window cleaning business on weekends. I didn't realize how dangerous that would be.

Soon Tyler had more business than he could handle on weekends. He asked his company if he could switch to four-day weeks. They agreed, but only if he put in the same hours as a five-day week.

Tyler started working 10 to 12 hours a day and washed windows three days a week. He no longer had the energy to get up two hours early for prayer and Scripture reading. He couldn't make his Celebrate Recovery meetings. He didn't have time for AA meetings or for meeting with his sponsor. He skipped church on Sundays and withdrew from all meaningful Christian relationships. When he drove his company vehicle to different appointments, he listened to country music.

It's not that Tyler did anything wrong. It's more that he stopped doing the right things and lost touch with his beliefs and his faith.

What happened to Tyler can be explained by the measuring cups below.

The first cup represents Tyler after he was born-again in a Minneapolis hospital and during 14 months at Metro Hope. God took up 80% of his life.

The second cup characterizes when Tyler left Metro Hope and started working for the cable company. All of a sudden, he had to deal with the natural things of the world that preoccupy all of us – work, food, housing, transportation, shopping, and such other things that came about when God booted Adam and Eve out of the Garden. Tyler now made up 50% of his life and God the other 50%. There are mature Christ-followers who have discovered the secret to incorporating God into even the most common things of their lives, but Tyler was a few hundred miles away from that point.

The third cup characterizes what happened when Tyler started the window-washing business and left Jesus several blocks away. He started drinking again so heavily that he blacked out three times driving his car. After the third time, he realized he needed to re-acquaint himself with Jesus or he'd be back in jail and hanging around railroad tracks again.

He quit his job, brought his car back to the dealership, and signed up for a stay at an Adult and Teen Challenge in Minnesota. I'm convinced he's now ready to follow Jesus so closely that he'll be hanging on to the back of His cloak.

I have a word of warning to those of you recovering from addictions or have been released from jail or prison. "The battle is never over."

You have the time in jail or a rehab facility to concentrate on Scripture reading, prayer, Bible studies, and Christian fellowship. You may think you're well equipped, but if you don't walk a step behind Jesus when you leave, you'll lose your way again.

But how do you do that? What I'm going to tell you next is action you can take to stay so close to Jesus that it'll look like you're twins.

Chapter Eleven
The Drip, Drip, Drip of the Holy Spirit

The San Joaquin Valley in Central California is roughly the size of Maryland and Massachusetts put together. It receives an average of 5 to 16 inches of water per year, yet is one of the most productive agricultural regions in the world, growing more than 250 crops. How can a near-desert be so fruitful? The answer can be summed up in one word – irrigation.

One method used extensively in the Valley is something called drip irrigation, which involves dripping water into the soil at very low rates close to plants so that only the part of the soil in which roots grow is wetted.

Your Way

Desert

God's Way

Fruitful Land

Let's take a drive down a highway that goes through the Valley. In spots, we'll see nothing but desert land alongside the road as far as the eye can see. In other places, we'll observe semi-arid land alongside the road and beyond that fertile fields growing grapes, lettuce, almonds, tomatoes, and 246 other crops.

Without Christ, you are that desert land where nothing of any value grows because no living water falls on you. If you accept Christ as your Savior but mainly go your own way and leave Him in the dust, you are the semi-arid land alongside the road. You let some of His living water fall on you, about enough to sustain vegetation of little value – cacti, evergreen brush, and small leafless plants.

Look beyond yourself and see the fertile fields inviting you to become part of them, where the living water continually soaks the land with the drip, drip, drip of the Holy Spirit and the fruits of the Holy Spirit grow within you.

When Tyler met the real Jesus, his spirit came alive and he experienced a whole new life where he could live without drugs and alcohol. But he needed a lot of nurturing of his new faith and received it during his 14-month stay at New Hope, where he received the living water of Jesus in the morning, in the afternoon, and in the evening. But then he moved away from God's nurturing water and ended up in semi-arid land.

I want to address three groups of you who are Christians struggling with addictions or crime or both. If you aren't a Christian yet, go back to Chapter Three.

1 FOR THOSE OF YOU IN A CHRISTIAN REHAB FACILITY, like Adult and Teen Challenge, you will have your faith nurtured for 13 months.

2 FOR THOSE OF YOU IN A JAIL OR PRISON, you have the time for your faith to be nurtured through reading Scripture, Bible studies, church services, praying, and fellowship with other believers. Some men and women in jails are among the strongest Christians I

know. I am heartened and encouraged to see men and women who are growing in faith every day.

3 FOR THOSE OF YOU WHO HAVE NEVER BEEN IN REHAB OR JAIL, you haven't had that separation time. Maybe you've made great progress with a therapist or counselor. Or you've had a spiritual awakening or have successfully drawn a line in the sand to separate the old you from the new you. But will it last?

All of you – and me too for that matter – are like grape vines in the San Juaquin Valley. We won't grow without the drip, drip, drip of the living water of the Holy Spirit. You can't just say, "I'm solid with the Lord Jesus Christ now and won't be having any more issues with addictions or criminal behavior."

If an orange tree doesn't get enough water, it will slowly become weaker and be subject to all the things in the environment that can do it harm –Sooty Mold, Root Rot, or Orangedog Caterpillars, to name a few.

If you don't have the steady drip, drip, drip of the Holy Spirit, you become weaker and subject to all the things that can do you harm – the temptations of Satan, the lures of the world, and the trials and tribulations that seem to attract you like a magnet.

You become under attack from the Sooty Mold of self-seeking gratification – think of unlawful sex or deadening your problems with drugs and alcohol. The Root Rot of corrupt friends and family muffle your commitment to live out your life for Christ. And the Orangedog Caterpillars of broken relationships, money problems, or being a person without a home to live in or a job to go to gnaw away at the very core of you.

I expect you have the picture by now. But if I end here, I've done nothing but heap bad news on you. I've done you no good unless I show you on a practical basis how to be nurtured by those drips of the Holy Spirit on a daily basis and avoid those things trying to destroy you.

1. SURRENDER. Your calling the shots in your life is what got you into trouble in the first place. Unless you trade masters from yourself to Jesus, the rest of this will do you about as much good as hanging around a pool hall.
2. READ SCRIPTURE DAILY. The Bible is the Word of God, authored by the Holy Spirit with a little help from his friends – Moses, King David, John, Paul, and a bunch of others. The Bible is not Jesus, but it points the way to Him. It is the living water Jesus talks about in the 4th Chapter of the Gospel of John.
3. PRAY CONTINUALLY. There is a simple pattern of prayer that is represented by the word ACTS.

    Adore, praise, and worship God throughout the day.

    Confess what you did the day before that went against God's commands and what you did not do to stay close to Him.

    Thank God for the blessings He has given you and the people He has put in your life to encourage you.

Supplication. Ask God for his blessings on you, your family and friends, and His help in upcoming trials, tribulations, and challenging events.
4. LEARN OFTEN – through preaching, teaching, Bible studies, Christian books, and other learning opportunities.
5. BE INVOLVED IN A SPIRIT-FILLED CHURCH. Not all of them are, you know. Do more than just show up on a Sunday. Join a small group, be an usher, help with clean-up projects, and other such things that allow you to rub shoulders with believers.
6. HANG AROUND CHRIST FOLLOWERS. There is a saying that you are who you hang around with. That should tell you enough why you want to spend time with your Christian brothers and sisters.
7. SERVE OTHERS IN CHRIST'S NAME. This is why I come to jails and Adult and Teen Challenge facilities. I need the drip, drip, drip myself or I will turn dry. So do you. Serve others whenever you can, and do it in the name of Jesus Christ.

Jail inmates, those in state or federal prisons, and addicts in a rehab facility have a priceless opportunity to find Jesus or rediscover the Jesus they have lost. These are the ones who come to Sunday afternoon Gideon Bible studies in the Wright County Jail. They are the ones who come to talks I give in county jails throughout Minnesota about how to stay out of jail. They are the ones I meet with one-to-one as a chaplain.

Too many of them, unfortunately, leave Jesus behind when they are released. They become the ones Jesus talked about in the parable of the sower. Some return to the well-traveled paths of this world, and birds sent by Satan eat them up. Some go back to rocky places without much soil or water, and they wither because they live in an arid wasteland. Some jump into the thorns of this world that choked them in the first place – gangs, dysfunctional families, criminal or addicted friends, and all sorts of situations and conditions that suck the spiritual life right out of them. And some continue being immersed in Jesus Christ and live in good soil when they get out of jail or a rehab facility. My purpose in visiting jails, rehab houses, and meeting with inmates is to help as many as I can fall on good soil in the outside world.

What I tell them is this: "Without the drip, drip, drip of the Holy Spirit, you are a semi-arid and infertile land where the coyotes howl and no good fruit lives."

If you leave Christ behind when you're released from Jail, He'll be waiting for you when you return. An inmate at the Wright County Jail

Chapter Twelve
The Heart of the Matter

Your self-worth comes from being united with Christ. The two of you become a team. But who is the leader and who the follower makes all the difference.

If you take the top spot in your heart, you're asking Jesus to trot along behind you and assist you in your battles. You want Him to take your side against the world, so to speak.

But Jesus isn't interested in following after you and cleaning up your messes. He wants you to follow Him. Letting Him do so is your best chance to do what you want to do instead of doing what you don't want to do.

You need to make this choice every hour of every day of every year. Don't be lazy in your commitment. As we found out with Tyler, the battle is never over. Joshua had it figured out in Joshua 24:15.

Choose for yourselves this day whom you shall serve...as for me and my household, we will serve the LORD.

The Prayer of Abandonment

Lord, I abandon myself to you today, desiring your Holy Spirit to rule my life, wanting you to fulfill Your mighty powers through me.

I acknowledge You in all my ways, leaning not on my own understanding but trusting You with all my heart, giving You my mind to think with, my will to decide, my emotions to react.

As of right now, I allow You, Lord Jesus, to govern my behavior wherever it may be - at home, at work, in recreation, at rest - rejoicing in the glorious fact that You live within me, sharing Your life with me, communicating that life to me, in the nitty-gritty process of being and living 24 hours a day.

Your breath in my lungs, Your words on my lips, Your smile on my face. Your vision through my eyes, Your understanding through my ears, Your touch with my hands.

What a marvelous thing, abiding like a branch on the vine, letting the vine bear the fruit through the branch. This is my prayer today, heavenly Father, quicken me to live it out, Your Spirit to my spirit, every minute of this day.

www.ingramcontent.com/pod-product-compliance
Lightning Source LLC
Chambersburg PA
CBHW050449010526
44118CB00013B/1748